The Mother Load

by V. Penn

MW01535196

0 43422 69590 4

Cover Illustration by Design Dynamics
Typography by MarketForce, Burr Ridge, IL

Published by Great Quotations Publishing Co.,
Glendale Heights, IL

Library of Congress Catalog Number: 98-75441

ISBN: 1-56245-356-4

Printed in Hong Kong

2

Dedication

"For The Migga."
Thanks!!

Introduction

On my Mother's more difficult days (of which, according to her, there were many), she always said the same thing: "Ya think it's easy?" Though punctuated with a question mark, this was rhetorical at best. That being the case, her trademark line still conjured up many possible replies. "Dusting doesn't necessarily look like a skill," and "I don't know, watching soap operas seems rather

leisurely" being among them. Truth be told, most lines mothers dish out seem ripe for reply and/or ridicule, and that's exactly what this book does. I'll be the first to translate and respond to exactly what Moms have been saying for years and years. More often than not, the "load" that they complain they are always carrying often appears to be a "load" of another sort.

But, then again, I *am* a guy.

"Make sure you wear your good underwear in case you're in an accident."

Laundry skills being called into question on top of a family tragedy is just plain too much.

"Beauty's only skin deep."

Sure, Ma. Hey, the UPS guy is here
with another case of wrinkle remover.

"Always say please and thank-you."

Then shouldn't you be saying, "Please always say please and thank-you. Thank-you."?

#1 MOM

"*Little girls are to be seen and not heard.*"

But, you're shrinking a little bit every day and getting louder every step of the way.

#1 MOM

"Honesty's the best policy."

Doesn't that apply to the credit card bill that you've been hiding from Dad for the last two months?

"As long as you're under my roof you'll live by my rules."

All right already, we'll watch what you want on TV.

"*Your face is going to freeze like that.*"

It's really getting to you, but you can't make a face back because you're the Mom, huh?

"*Use your head.*"

**Like when you locked the keys in the car?
While it was running?**

"Because I'm the Mother, that's why."

Just plain out of reasons, aren't you?

14

"Will there be any parents there?"

No, you don't have to chaperone.

"Nobody likes a sore loser."

I was thinking just that the other night when you threw your slippers at the television during the Lotto drawing.

"Self-praise stinks."

I know. By the way, your gold-plated "#1 Mom" necklace is gorgeous!

"I've got eyes in the back of my head."

**Too tired to actually watch me today,
so just plant the seeds of paranoia, huh?**

MOM'S TAXI

"Put on a sweater if you're cold."

Fuel prices go up?

"What do I have to do to get you to keep your room clean and tidy?"

Stop sending me to it all the time for starters.

#1 MOM

"If all your friends jumped off a cliff would you do that, too?"

No. And I wouldn't drive off one, either, in the mini-van you talked Dad into buying after everyone you know all bought one.

#1 MOM

"If at first you don't succeed try, try again."

Yet that doesn't apply to me expressing myself artistically on the kitchen wall, now, does it?

"You're too big to sleep with Mommy and Daddy anymore."

You didn't say that two nights ago. Then again, you were wearing much bigger pajamas then, too.

"Don't waste such a beautiful day cooped up in the house."

New Lifetime Movie for Women premiering today, is there?

"*You are what you eat.*"

Well, it's not like a gigantic Triscuit is telling me this, so...

"Smile and the whole
world smiles with you."

Oh, are we going to the supermarket today?

COOKIES

26

"It's not polite to swear."

**Even the word I got from you
the other night when that
telemarketer called?**

27

"What do we say when
someone gives us something?"

**Well, they gave it to <u>me</u>, and evidently,
"Just what I wanted!" isn't the correct answer.**

"Finish your milk like Mommy always does."

But, Mommy gets to give hers cool names like "White Russian."

"Respect your elders."

Sure! Let Grandma out of her room and I'll tell her I love her.

"Call me if you're going to be late."

I will. And, by the way, my diary goes in the top drawer, not the second.

MOM'S TAXI

"*I raised you better than that.*"

Everyone _is_ looking, aren't they?

"No swimming for at least 45 minutes after lunch or you'll get cramps.

Wanna get a little sun, do we?

#1 MOM

"Your body is a temple."

So, you've hit a temple with a wooden spoon before?

"Don't spill anything on the carpet."

Vacuuming's no way to spend a Saturday night.

"No friends over while we're gone."

**Nothing like a missed opportunity
to use outdated phrases and
teach ancient dance steps.**

"No supper for you."

What, Ma? I can't hear you over the smoke detector going off!

"Do as I say, not as I do."

**Two of us arguing with Daddy
cuts the chances of winning to half.**

"*Look at me when I'm talking to you.*"

**Seeking confirmation on if
the child is laughing.**

"Zip up your jacket before you catch cold."

Look as geeky as possible and maybe dating can be put off another two years.

"I'll wash your mouth out with soap."

Wouldn't that defy the very logic behind child-proof bottles, for example?

"Did you forget that you have a curfew?"

**The only thing more embarrassing than that
is the music you make us listen to when
you drive me and my friends to the mall,
so whadda you think?**

MOM'S TAXI

"*Don't forget to leave cookies for Santa.*"

Could you do that, Ma?
You always seem to pick
the kind that he really likes!

MOM'S TAXI

"No dessert tonight for you."

Particularly proud of the pudding this time around, are we?

#1 MOM

"*Did you do all your homework?*"

**Yeah, I suppose the conversation
is veering towards sex.**

#1 MOM

"Stop fighting with your brothers and sisters."

That kinda clashes with this afternoon's "Stick up for yourself" lesson a little, doesn't it, Ma? Besides, I wonder what Aunt Mary's take on that belief would be.

46

"If your father says it's okay."

Dad <u>has</u> been the good guy for a while, hasn't he?

"*You've got a great personality.*"

Parent-speak for "you're ugly."

"Growing old is easy;
the hard part is growing up."

**Where were those words of wisdom
during your first brown spot sighting?**

"It wasn't like that when
I was your age."

**I have no idea how to help
you with this problem.**

50

"Don't sit so close to the TV."

Oh, I'm blocking you.

"You can do much better
if you apply yourself."

**Those PTA meetings <u>are</u>
quite often aren't they?**

"Your new friend is a bad influence."

No, I guess you and I haven't been spending much time together.

"Don't use that tone with me."

The #1 perk of being a mom is using the tone so naturally they're going to be possessive over it.

"I'll deal with you when I get off the telephone!"

News flash in the Neighborhood Cheating Department!

"*Nobody wants the cow when they can get the milk for free.*"

Seriously, Ma, who wants a cow anyway?

#1 MOM

"You're punished until the cows come home!"

Unless you live on a farm this is an open-ended punishment -- a true parental trick!

"Close the door; this isn't a barn."

Hey, I'm a little confused, what with the "punished 'til the cows come home" and "nobody wants the cow when they can get the milk for free" stuff.

"*You got that from your Father.*"

**Then it's obviously not a good thing.
Those seem to come directly from you.**

"There had to be mold
growing in your bedroom."

*I thought they broke the mold
when you had me, Ma.*

"*Don't make me tell you a second time.*"

*I didn't want to hear it the first time,
so I don't seem to have much to do with it.*

"It's what's inside that counts."

Really dry meat loaf?

"You made your bed, now lie in it."

But I didn't wanna make it.
You kept going on and on about it!

"*Act your age.*"

20 minutes late for curfew
at 16 _is_ acting your age!

"Don't put all your eggs in one basket."

Well, why do you keep putting all those egg <u>shells</u> in my breakfast?

"The apple doesn't fall far from the tree."

Jeez, it bounced clear across the street the last time I got a report card.

"One mother can take care of 100 kids, but 100 kids can't take care of one mother."

Yet my birthday parties are limited to 6.

"*Are you listening to me?*"

Trick question. Could result in much more conversation than you bargained for.

#1 MOM

"Don't be such a handful."

**Four years of "So-o-o-o big"
resulting in nothing but smiles
and handfuls are a bad thing.**

#1 MOM

"It's all fun and games
until somebody gets hurt."

**Motherhood 101.
As obvious a statement
as "The stove is hot."**

"You should marry someone just like me."

I don't think there are menopausal people my age.

"Father knows best."

**He usually does when you have
a glass of wine in your hand.**

"You could do it my way happy or your way sad."

Let me get this straight: Taking my little brother on the date with me is the <u>happy</u> way?

"*Wash behind your ears.*"

I wouldn't have to if you weren't so intent on my getting such bad haircuts!

"Don't play with matches."

**This from the chain-smoking
late night TV fan!**

"*I may know more about it than you think.*"

Uh oh, nostalgia alert!
Yearbook could be pulled from the closet!

"People in glass houses
shouldn't throw stones."

I was thinking that the other day when
you criticized my jeans and T-shirt
while you were wearing that
plastic purple sweat suit.

"A fool and his money are soon parted."

Well, that fool should stop leaving his wallet in his golf bag every Tuesday when you go to Bingo.

MOM'S TAXI

"Don't spoil your dinner with snacks."

The concept of appetizers eludes most parents.

"Do you know how many hours of labor I went through with you?"

The limitless bargaining chip.

#1 MOM

"That's not music. It's noise."

The statement that is an opening act for Varicose veins.

#1 MOM

81

"*Stop playing with your food.*"

Maybe if you did a bit more before you deemed it ready, it wouldn't seem like such a novelty.

"It's time we had a talk about the birds and the bees."

Ah, so that's why Dad's stopped hugging me!

"*Why don't you take some time for yourself until you do understand.*"

Variation of the "Go to your room" theme.

"Take your shoes off before you come in this house."

Will you do the same with your slippers the next time you come to my school?

"*Don't answer a question with a question.*"

Even when 90% of what you ask me makes me think, "What are you talking about?"

"You can pick your friends,
but you can't pick your family."

Let's meet your date!

"You have a lot of explaining to do."

Massive bluff. Possible telephone call to a friend's house, but came up empty.

"You don't know how lucky you are. You should have had Grandma for a mother."

The lady who does nothing but feed me and pays me every time I visit her? Yeah, that must've been tough.

"I hope you have kids who are just like you."

Well, it would make deciding what to watch on TV and what to listen to in the car a no-brainer.

MOM'S TAXI

"I'm the one who keeps this family together."

**Remember that next time
you and Daddy almost divorce
over putting up the Christmas tree.**

MOM'S TAXI

"Don't let the bed bugs bite."

A year and a half to shake my imaginary friend and there are bed bugs!?

#1
MOM

"You're eating me out of house and home."

Well, you shoulda slowed up on the "finish your vegetables" routine.

#1 MOM

"Keep your fingers crossed."

Why, are you going to make me promise something?

"*The secret to any good relationship is communication.*

**The non-confrontational
"We need to have a long talk."**

"No fighting at the dinner table."

**She's in a bad enough mood
from having to cook it.**

"Grab the tiger by the tail."

Yet, not the cat or you're punished."

"Only the best for you."

**Then can you explain
the hand-me-downs?**

"It's going to be a long, hot summer."

The countdown to Mommy blowing her stack has begun.

"When I was your age,
I used to walk five miles to school."

So you won't be driving me then...

"I helped my mother clean every day when I was a kid."

Then you should be great at it now.

"*Your teacher says you've been having a tough time in school.*"

Correct me if I'm wrong, but you <u>are</u> the one always telling me that I should be doing my homework, aren't you?

MOM'S TAXI

"Quiet in church!"

Sorry, but it's not like we're here more than once a year.

MOM'S TAXI

"*Wait until your father hears about this.*"

The parental version of "I'm tellin'."

"Rome wasn't built in a day."

But I gotta clean up that bedroom in one shot, huh?

#1 MOM

"*Laugh and the world laughs with you.*"

Where was that cliche when I wound up in detention for that funny outburst in class?

"You're not going out of the house like that, are you?

Well, let's see: friends are out front honking the horn, I ran down the stairs, I'm opening the front door...

"*You can tell me anything.*"

Virgin status in question.

"It's all fun and games until someone gets hurt."

Oh, I don't know; football and hockey remain game-like even through the injuries.

"You grew overnight."

Shouldn't we be having this conversation at the mall then?

"You were such a good baby."

And Dad was such a romantic, too, huh? Ever notice the common denominator in both of these past-tense situations is you?

"Being the mom is the toughest job there is."

As I'm reminded every May.

"That's not what you're going to wear, is it?"

Yup. And now I know it's right on the money.

"We'll make ends meet."

**"We'll?" Last week I remember all
I'm responsible for around here
is the garbage once a week!**

"Doesn't Mommy always know
what to get you for Christmas?

Not judging by this snowman-covered scarf!

"There's no place like home."

Why do you think I never wanted to go to school?

"Let Mommy kiss it
and make it better."

**Can't do that with a
report card, though, huh?**

#1 MOM

"*You could put an eye out.*"

With a nerf ball? If you want me to stop running just say so.

"Edward Francis O'Neil,
get in this house this second!!"

Full name alert. Big trouble!

"Be careful what you wish for!"

Where was that disclaimer as everyone stood around me while I almost had asthma attacks blowing candles my whole life?

"I'm just a mother."

Funny how that can be an apology as well as a reason why I can't do certain things and wonder why.

"We need to have a long talk."

In other words, you have quite a few questions for me.

"I've been slaving over a hot stove all day."

Oprah was a repeat?

"*You don't know how lucky you are.*"

Well, that should concern you!
Is it because you send me to my room
too often, or because you never let
me do what I want to do, or...

"If you can't stand the heat,
get out of the kitchen."

**But, then who will dice
the vegetables for you?**

"*He who hesitates is lost.*"

What's that? I was just jotting down your "patience is a virtue" bit from last night's "you can't go on a car date until you're 18" talk.

"What will be will be."

Mom on a philosophical day.
Translation: No, you can't.

"*Can't you read between the lines?*"

**Would we be having
this exchange if I could?**

#1
MOM

"Two heads are better than one."

Yet, I have to do my math myself.

#1 MOM

"Be good to your brothers and sisters; they're the only ones you have."

**Dad's the only husband you have
and how good could sleeping
on the couch possibly be?**

"*Now, now, your teacher doesn't hate you.*"

Probably not, but my hating <u>him</u> really isn't a good excuse for doing lousy in his class.

"The early bird catches the worm."

**Evidently there're no worms around
on Christmas morning then, huh?**

"No child of mine behaves like that."

Mom, excuse me, but I just did behave like that. That's why you've been called down here.

"If you swallow a seed the watermelon will grow inside of you.

No problem. I disregard your "don't swallow your gum" thing so much the seed'll just stick to a bone or something.

"Don't look a gift horse in the mouth."

**Even when it's not a horse,
but a pair of slipper-socks instead?**

"I carried you for nine months!"

I'm sure that most children
would agree that that's a card
Moms should use on Dads.

"You need a slice of humble pie."

This coming from a woman with a "Best Mom on Board" bumper sticker on the back of her car!

"*Don't spend your allowance in one place.*"

Gee, then I hope I don't run into anyone selling the newspaper!

"*You don't need one of these.*"

And you **needed** that pewter egg that's on the mantel?

"*You don't know what labor is.*"

Danger -- "Nine months" rant coming!!

#1 MOM

"*You're going to college.*"

Translation: You're moving out at 18.

#1 MOM

"They're just jealous."

Of what exactly -- my pocket protector?

"*Your curfew's 11, not 11:05.*"

Ever heard of a snooze alarm?

"Rinse your plate off before putting it in the dishwasher."

Wouldn't that be like heating up a snack before putting it in the oven?

"Stop touching it or it will get worse."

A theory that doesn't extend to homework.

"Practice what you preach."

What's that, Ma? I can't understand you with the licorice in your mouth exactly 20 minutes before dinner.

"*Mommy sees everything.*"

**Then why do you keep asking me
what I do after school every day?**

"It's all over but the shouting!"

A mother's battle cry.

"If he loves you he'll wait."

You tell him that, because talking to you about sex has made <u>me</u> lose interest, so...

"*You're not a baby anymore.*"

**I know, Ma. That's why we fight
over me having girls in my room.**

"Watch your mouth."

How can I when you tell me to stop looking in the mirror so much?

MOM'S TAXI

"*Half a loaf is better than none.*"

**Why do I always hear that one
on the days when you've forgotten
I'm having friends over for dinner?**

#1
MOM

"Every cloud has a silver lining."

A scarce sentiment when I get detention.

"Anything happen in school today?"

Nope. So do I have to go again tomorrow?

"*If you walk out that door you better keep on walking!*"

Well, I wasn't planning on moving onto the front lawn!

"What do you want to be when you grow up?"

Someone who doesn't begin asking their child that question when they're six, actually.

"What's the movie that you're going to see about?

Possible review expected. At least research a family-oriented film to report back on.

"What's your hand doing in the cookie jar?

Is this a trick question?

COOKIES

"I used to get up at 3am to feed you!"

And why did that stop exactly?

"Life isn't fair."

Well, now, that just ups the drama level, doesn't it?

"Don't forget your lunch."

**It's been the same every day
since first grade! How could I?**

"Sweet 16 and never been kissed."

That's rhetorical, right?

"You're not old enough."

Yet, I've been old enough to drag
a massive lawn mower across
the yard since I was 10.

"I'll help you pack."

**Because you're obsessive compulsive,
not because you're frustrated.**

#1 MOM

"*Home is where the heart is.*"

So if I looked the word up in a thesaurus I'd find the words chores, punishment, and squabbles there?

#1 MOM

"*What you see is what you get.*"

You, Dad, the station wagon, and your Motown tape? Cool!

"If you don't have something good to say, don't say anything at all.

Other Titles by Great Quotations

301 Ways to Stay Young At Heart
African-American Wisdom
A Lifetime of Love
A Light Heart Lives Long
Angel-grams
As A Cat Thinketh
A Servant's Heart
Astrology for Cats
Astrology for Dogs
A Teacher is Better Than Two Books
A Touch of Friendship
Can We Talk
Celebrating Women
Chicken Soup
Chocoholic Reasonettes
Daddy & Me
Dare to Excel
Erasing My Sanity
Falling in Love
Fantastic Father, Dependable Dad
Golden Years, Golden Words
Graduation Is Just The Beginning
Grandma, I Love You
Happiness is Found Along The Way

High Anxieties
Hooked on Golf
I Didn't Do It
Ignorance is Bliss
I'm Not Over the Hill
Inspirations
Interior Design for Idiots
Let's Talk Decorating
Life's Lessons
Life's Simple Pleasures
Looking for Mr. Right
Midwest Wisdom
Mommy & Me
Mom's Homemade Jams
Mother, I Love You
Motivating Quotes for Motivated People
Mrs. Murphy's Laws
Mrs. Webster's Dictionary
My Daughter, My Special Friend
Only a Sister
Parenting 101
Pink Power
Read the Fine Print

Reflections
Romantic Rhapsody
Size Counts !
Social Disgraces
Sports Prose
Stress or Sanity
The ABC's of Parenting
The Be-Attitudes
The Birthday Astrologer
The Cornerstones of Success
The Rose Mystique
The Secret Language of Men
The Secret Language of Women
The Secrets in Your Face
The Secrets in Your Name
TeenAge of Insanity
Thanks from the Heart
The Lemonade Handbook
The Mother Load
The Other Species
Wedding Wonders
Words From The Coach
Working Woman's World

Great Quotations Publishing Company
1967 Quincy Court
Glendale Heights, IL 60139, U.S.A.
Phone: 630-582-2800   Fax: 630-582-2813
http://www.greatquotations.com